Shades of Childhood
Children's Stories For Grownups

BY

JUNE IRENE ANDERSON

ILLUSTRATIONS BY CARYN INDERLEE

ISBN: 0-75962-231-0

This book is printed on acid free paper.

1stBooks - rev. 05/10/01

A FAMILY LEGACY

In looking back over my childhood years from the vantage point of advanced adulthood, I realize now, in an age when "dysfunction" seems to be the buzzword, that if there was anything unique about the Gossler family, it was its normalcy. Dad went to work every day and came home to his family every evening. Mom stayed home every day (one job, one-car families were the norm) cooked, cleaned, and ministered to the affairs of her daughters. The biggest household issues revolved around eating our vegetables and whose turn it was to do the dishes.

Raising their children in an era before "experts" and the "Information Age," my parents' world and perspectives were limited to their own experiences and instincts. They didn't have all of the answers (nor were there so many questions back then in the forties and fifties), but Mom and Dad were hard working, straight-shooting, clean-living people. They were devoted to each other and dedicated to the care and nurture of their five daughters of whom I am the oldest.

Each story in this book was triggered by some current event or situation that brought back memories of this relatively short, but overwhelmingly important era of my lifespan. While many of these stories are based on my own childhood memories, one reaches back into my father's childhood, one is a souped-up tall-tale drawn from my son's childhood, and one is a contemporary event for reading to my grandchildren. They are all true (to some degree more or less).

Shades of Childhood spans the generations from the Model T Ford to Virtual Reality. It is an eclectic collection of funny little feel-good stories tied together by the grandmas and the grandpas, the aunts and the uncles, the sisters and the Cousin, and especially the Mom and Dad whose love and commitment to each other and to us created this uniquely "normal" family.

THANKS FOR THE MEMORIES

Thanks to my mom and dad, Lois and Clarence Gossler, my sisters, Pat Young, Gail Kishish, JoAnn Pierson, and Laurie Malone, and especially Cousin Judy for being such an important part of these memories. And thanks to my husband Roger, my children, Terri Thompson, Dale, Todd, and Jack Anderson, their spouses and children for giving these memories meaning.

Also… Thanks, Pat and Sue for proofing the copy, Caryn for your wonderful illustrations, Dale for the scans, and Roger for your love and support in all I do.

There once was a father named Clarence

Who brought up five girls with forbearance.

He $uffered through braces

And make-up on faces.

He's a heck of a half of a parence.

...............June

There once was a mother named Lois

Who loved us and fed us and clothed us.

Now that we're grown

And have kids of our own

We marvel at the great job she done us.

(Except our English ain't too hot.)

……….JoAnn

This Book is dedicated to them.

CONTENTS

Memories are distilled in the recesses of the mind,

taking on meaning in the passageways of time.

THE $2.00 WEDDING

"I now pronounce you man and wife my fee is $2.00" and in one run-on sentence my parents were married by a justice of the peace in Brookings, South Dakota. It was Depression Days, March 25, 1936, and the wedding had to be kept secret lest my mother lose her job at the University. Jobs were scarce and were rationed—one to a family.

At that time my father was working as a salesman for Northern States Power Company selling large appliances, such as stoves and refrigerators, to those who could afford them. Part of his value to the Power Company was the load-building component of his work. By selling these energy-consuming appliances he created the need for more electrical usage, which necessitated more electrical runs into households that were short on that commodity, thus generating more revenue for the electric company.

Despite hard times Mother had completed a two-year degree program in dental hygiene. She was fortunate to have found part-time work in her field at the University of Minnesota. Sometimes she was also able to fill in for her sister, Doris, at their father's electric store. Grandpa Annis sold electrical appliances and, as an electrician, also did the wiring.

My father, Clarence, often had need of an electrician to install the additional wiring for his customers. He had been using the services of Grandpa's competitor until he learned the reason for so many of his sales falling through. The electrician he was recommending to his customers would talk them into canceling their order with NSP and buying the appliance from his store instead. Ironically, this same electrician had started out in the electrical business working for my grandpa. He was fired when Grandpa discovered he was using time and materials, courtesy of Annis Electric Company, to wire jobs he had contracted for himself on the side.

On a day that was to set the stage for the future, Clarence walked into Annis Electric to talk with the owner, C.B. Annis, about installing the wiring for his customers. The first person he encountered was C.B.'s beautiful twenty-three year old daughter Lois typing away on the old Underwood. Lois was the youngest of Carlton Bruce and Cora Annis's four children. When Lois had turned eighteen and graduated from high school her parents did the unthinkable. They got divorced! Cora married the "other man" in her life almost immediately, establishing a new home for herself in which Lois felt unwelcome. C.B. retained the family house, but shared it with Doris, her husband, and two children. There was no place for Lois there, either. She spent several unhappy years, rootless and alone, living with friends and fending for herself.

Thirty-two year old Clarence had also encountered the Dirty D word—his own divorce many years earlier. Following the break-up of his short marriage, he had moved back into the family home where he lived with his folks and his unmarried brother and sister.

How big a role does coincidence play in the events of our lives? A fatal misstep that can end a life prematurely? Or a chance encounter that leads to a permanent relationship with results reaching far into the future? It seems as if the Fates had conspired to place Lois and Clarence in the same place at the same time. Brought together by a crooked contractor and a mutual need for each other, they experienced the proverbial "love at first sight" and the rest is history—our family history.

****

And what of the $2.00 investment paid so long ago to a justice of the peace in Brookings, South Dakota? To date it has netted 5 daughters, 6 granddaughters, 8 grandsons, 21 great-grandchildren, lots of warm and happy memories and lots of love. What a bargain!

MEMORABLE DOLLS OF MY CHILDHOOD

OR

THE LAST LAUGH

How well I remember my first doll, Baby Cry Aloud Blink A Lot. It had a soft cloth body with a moan box in its belly that emitted a distressing cry when moved, and a molded plastic head with blue eyes that popped open when it sat up and closed when it lay down. Mother had given my little sister Patty and me what amounted to a matched pair on that long ago Christmas. Patty loved her doll and played with it by the hour. I hated mine. I had wanted a Lionel Electric Train Set.

The next Christmas Mother gave both of us Betsy Wetsy Baby Dolls. Patty was intrigued with the whole process. Stick a baby bottle full of water (other liquid not recommended by manufacturer) in the mouth hole. Let gravity do its work.

Eureka! A wet diaper on the other end to change. How disgusting. I had begged for a puppy.

Undaunted by her failure to please her errant daughter, Mother gave us each a Baby Creeper the next year. Wind it up. Put it on the floor. Watch it undulate from side to side just like a real baby. Positively creepy. I had asked for a pair of skis with real bindings.

Three strikes and out was not part of Mother's game plan. This had become an unacknowledged Battle of Wills. "Girls are supposed to play with dolls," Mother insisted. "I played with dolls when I was a girl. Your sister plays with dolls."

Determined that I, her oldest daughter and partial namesake, would also come to love and treasure at least one of these icons of girlhood, Mother thought she'd up her batting average by tempting me with The Ultimate—a Magic Skin Doll. Unlike dolls with cloth or plastic bodies, this enticing creature had the feel of real flesh due to the soft rubber skin encasing a foam rubber body. "It is," Mother informed me, "State of The Art Technology in the doll industry." Gross. I had been hoping for a Giant Erector Set.

My childhood days were running their course and I was fast approaching puberty. On my twelfth birthday Mother made one last desperate attempt to awaken the dormant doll gene that lay sleeping in my psyche. Having read an article dealing with that new phenomenon, Child Psychology, she concocted a cure for my doll phobia, something that, according to the testimonial on the package, would "appeal to girls of all ages." The cure was a Storybook Doll, a five-inch china figurine dressed in the national costume of the Netherlands.

Now, maybe Mother had finally worn me down, or maybe I was just becoming more sensitive in my advancing years. I accepted the authentically dressed miniature doll without complaint and put it on my shelf where I could look at it, but didn't have to play with it. Having finally struck paydirt, Mother followed up successive Christmases and birthdays with Miss Netherlands's Swedish, English, Swiss, French, Polish, Irish, Spanish, and Norwegian sisters which kept each other company on my shelf for many years and, hopefully, were increasing in value as collectors' items as promised in the promotional.

Relentlessly, the generational cycle keeps rolling along. In another ten years I found myself in my mother's shoes, married with a little girl of my own. My mother, the Keeper of Memories and Giver of Dolls, had one last present from the past for her grownup daughter. With all due ceremony she presented me with a large, lovingly wrapped box. "It's a memento of your childhood," she said. "I've been saving it all these years for you to pass on to your own child."

Visualizing my lost and scattered Storybook Dolls together once again to undoubtedly make me rich as their value on the collectors' market had increased substantially, I opened the package—and what to my wondering eyes should appear but the Magic Skin Doll lying undisturbed after all these years, still in its original box. "The rest of your castoff dolls were all loved to pieces by your sister," Mother explained, "but I put this one away for you until you got old enough to appreciate it."

Now I know that Mother's motives were pure when she set aside that one special doll from my childhood, and in a perverse way her unwitting choice couldn't have been more appropriate or symbolic. Dutifully, I lifted the Magic Skin Doll from its box to show to my baby daughter. As if in retaliation for its years of neglect, the rubber foam that was the essence of this unloved, unwanted doll disintegrated at my touch, leaking out through cracks in the lifelike rubber skin to settle in powdery piles all over the three of us. The last of Mother's Memorable Dolls was history.

To this day Mother and I have found absolutely no trace of the now priceless Storybook Dolls. But in my heart of hearts, I know that somewhere in the Heavenly Kingdom of Dolls the rejects from my childhood have all gotten together to have the last laugh.

THE GREAT GOLDFISH CAPER

I learned early in life that it's easier to beg forgiveness than ask permission. My parents' standing answer to most requests was an automatic "no." "No, you don't need it." "No, you can't have it." "No, you can't go." Whining and begging served no useful purpose and, as a strategy, tended to irritate them. "I said 'no' and I mean it. If you keep it up, you're gonna get a spanking."

Therefore, if I really wanted something, it was better to take matters into my own hands. Do what had to be done, and let my parents deal with the consequences. Such was the case with the goldfish caper. Furry, feathered, or finny, I was attracted to anything that crawled, ran, flew or swam, but my efforts to bring any such creature into the house were always met by an emphatic "NO! Get it out of here," from my mother. I knew

13

stealth would have to be involved if we were to become the proud possessors of goldfish.

Every time I accompanied my mother downtown I lingered longingly in the pet department of the five and dime store watching the glittering goldfish swim in their sparkling, spacious aquariums. I was determined to buy a pair, but I would have to wait for the golden opportunity. The target date was our annual family Christmas shopping expedition. For months I had frugally saved every quarter of my twenty-five cent weekly allowance in anticipation of this annual event.

The big day finally arrived. Mom and Dad bundled the four of us up into the Dodge and off we headed to Dayton's Department Store. Dad parked the car in the Dayton garage and we escalated up to the eighth floor auditorium. My sisters and I joined the long line of children waiting to see Santa Claus with out parents proudly watching our progress. We capped off our

Dayton's holiday visit with a ride on a miniature train through a winter wonderland of artificial snow laden pine trees arching over the train track.

After our Christmas adventure we headed to the five and dime where we girls could do some affordable shopping. My sisters made a bee-line for the toy department with my parents in tow. Mom and Dad knew they had their work cut out for them, trying to convince their daughters that they were supposed to spend their money on gifts for others, not toys for themselves.

I saw my golden opportunity and slipped away to the pet department a few aisles away. After making sure I was unobserved by any family members, I caught the attention of the fish clerk. "I'd like two goldfish," I said pointing to the two that had caught my fancy. "I also want a goldfish bowl and some fish food."

The clerk obligingly scooped the two fish into the catch net and deposited them in a small water-filled carton that resembled the cardboard container for Chinese take-out. She put the goldfish carton into one paper bag; the bowl and food she put into another. A quarter apiece for the two goldfish, a quarter for a goldfish bowl, and ten cents for fish food. I nervously counted my money into the outstretched hand of the store clerk. This transaction was taking way too long. Holding my breath, I checked the aisle for any sign of family members coming to fetch me back into the fold.

"Do you have city water?" the clerk asked as she handed me the goldfish.

"Of course we have water," I replied, anxious to be on my way. She said something else about water, but I was too distracted with the possibility of being caught to pay her much attention.

Mom and Dad were still busy with my little sisters when I returned to the toy department. They smiled at me as I slipped my purchases into the shopping bag, thinking I had done some Christmas shopping on my own.

Shopping with my sisters was a little more difficult for them.

"No, you can't have that," insisted my mother.

"You came here to buy presents for each other, not yourself," my dad told another stubborn sister.

"Now stop that whining, or you're going to get it," said my mother.

Finally, the gift buying was completed and the shopping bag filled. We headed back to Dayton's garage to retrieve our car. It was a pleasure to rest our shop-weary bones on the hard wooden bench while we waited for the parking attendant to locate our vehicle and bring it to us. Dad was holding my littlest sister, JoAnn, on his lap. Mom was holding the shopping bag on hers. Suddenly, a strange look came over her face. She felt her lap. She felt the bag. They were both wet!

"How can this be?!" she exclaimed.

Setting the bag down on the bench, she took the packages out one by one. At the bottom was a very wet paper bag. Inside the bag was what appeared to be a carton of Chinese take-out. Further examination revealed it to be a container with two goldfish flopping around in the inch of water left in the bottom. The rest had leaked out.

"Where's the bathroom?" Mother demanded of the cashier. She grabbed the carton and headed in the direction the cashier was pointing.

I started to cry. Oh no. Not the toilet!

Mother returned about the same time our car materialized outside the waiting area. She was holding the goldfish carton by its metal handle. Obviously, it had been refilled, for some water was still leaking out the bottom.

"Hand me the bowl," she said.

With shaking hands I did as I was told.

She put the carton inside the bowl. "Now hold on to that and don't drop it."

We all piled into the car and headed home.

Well, my mission was accomplished. I got the goldfish into the house, and Mom didn't say "no." Instead she asked about the water. "Did the clerk say city water was okay to use?"

"She said something about water," I replied. "I guess she said it was okay."

We filled the bowl from the tap and watched the two hydrated fish happily swimming around in their new home. Then I got ready for bed and went to say goodnight to my finny friends. To my horror one of them was floating upside-down, the other gasping for air.

Again, Mother sized up the situation and took fast action. "Clarence," she said to my father. "Drive over to Windom Park and pump up some well water." She handed my dad a bucket.

While Dad was on his errand of mercy Mom and I kept vigil over the surviving goldfish. "I think the clerk was trying to tell you that you couldn't use city water for your goldfish," she explained. "City water is chlorinated to kill germs and make it safe for drinking. Unfortunately, it also kills fish."

Luckily, Dad arrived back home with the life-saving water before the remaining goldfish expired. It recuperated from its near brush with death, but looked so lonesome that Mother suggested we buy another one to keep it company. That was the first in a long succession of goldfish. Our family had found a hobby, and nobody said, "No."

June Irene Anderson

CHRISTMAS NIGHTIES

Mother was the tradition maker in our family. Dad happily went along for the ride. Christmas, the high holiday in our household, was already rich with festive traditions, trimming the tree, hanging our stockings, opening presents, and Santa Claus. I guess Mother was a 1940's era feminist, for she thought there should be one more tradition—Christmas nighties for her daughters. And that's how Mrs. Santa got into the act.

Every year as the holiday approached, our house became a beehive of activity; cleaning, shopping, decorating, cooking, and sewing. For weeks before Christmas, my sisters and I would lay in bed listening to Mother's sewing machine humming its clackety song long into the evening. Somehow, she always had a lot of mending to do at that time of year.

Christmas Eve Day marked the beginning of the festivities that would last well into the next day. After dinner was eaten and the dishes done, Pat, Gail, JoAnn, and I would begin our Christmas nightie vigil, waiting for Mrs. Santa to magically appear and lay our nightgowns out on our double beds. One year we spent the better part of Christmas Eve hiding behind a big dresser in our shared bedroom. We were hoping to catch her in the act. Finally, out of sheer boredom, we returned downstairs to rejoin Mom and Dad, but we continued to check that upstairs bedroom at strategic intervals.

The evening wore on, but no nighties appeared. We were getting worried. Where was Mrs. Santa? Had she forgotten us? Finally, Dad took pity and brought us into the kitchen for some hot chocolate. The next time we checked, the nighties had miraculously arranged themselves on our bed pillows. Mrs. Santa had come after all!

CHRISTMAS AND THE NAUGHTY ONE

When I was a little girl we celebrated Christmas with my father's family which included Cousin Judy, the adopted daughter of Dad's sister Irene, and the only resident cousin on this side of the family. Judy's father had dropped dead at work one day, and my aunt had transferred the sum total of her affection to their daughter. In Aunt Irene's eyes Judy could do no wrong. In my mother's eyes Judy was a spoiled brat who talked back to her elders and sassed her own mother.

Three year older than I, Judy was very bossy, but my younger sisters and I knew it was in our best interest to yield to her dictatorial tendencies. Without Cousin Judy routine family visits between relatives could be very dull. But with Judy we were privy to big kid stuff. While the adults droned on in the living room, she would spirit us away to a bedroom to show us boxesful of treasure and confide earsful of secrets. If one were fortunate enough to be invited to spend the night at Judy's house, she could anticipate a day of don't-tell-your-parents adventure. Cousin Judy was fearless. She was excitement. She could make things happen.

On the drive home from these Sunday get-togethers, my parents would sit in the front seat of the car discussing Judy's latest bout of bratty behavior.

"And she told your mother that her legs work and to use them and get her own glass of water!"

"She said that to her own grandmother? What a brat! I'm sure our girls would never say anything like that."

And I would sit in the back seat uncomfortably reviewing my own faults and shortcomings, hoping they weren't grist for someone else's family discussion.

Although my paternal relatives celebrated Christmas Day at our house, Christmas itself began weeks earlier, punctuated by the jingling of sleighbells signaling one of Santa's numerous preseason visits, the purpose of which, Mother informed us, was to see if we were behaving ourselves. One year he made a post-Christmas visit to take back my toy-typewriter-that-almost-works-like-a-real-one, just as Mother had warned me he would do if I didn't start minding her. Mother needed all the help she could get to keep order in the house while my sisters and I raced from one Christmas task to another.

We took our gift buying seriously, agonizing long minutes in the five and dime trying to find the perfect twenty-five to thirty-nine cent gifts for the grownups—the yearly ashtray for our non-smoking uncle, painted plaster dogs made in Occupied Japan for the aunts, and a five by seven inch tinny-gold picture frame with a slinky Hollywood actress glaring provocatively at its intended recipient, our aged grandmother.

We wrapped their gifts in the scraps of paper and Christmas stickers and ribbon Mother saved from year to year. We wrapped gifts for each other in secret and unwrapped the ones with our names on in double secrecy. We explored closets and cubbyholes and crawled under the beds in our search for unsecured presents.

We trimmed the tree and untrimmed the tree and argued over retrimming the tree until we heard the warning jingle of Santa's sleighbells. We visited the department store Santas and were unfazed by the multiplicity of the red-suited ones. "Stand-ins for the real Santa who is very busy at the North Pole right now," Dad had explained. Assuring each Santa in turn that we were practically perfect children, we gave them handwritten copies of our "What I Want for Christmas" lists. We hung our stockings on the bedposts Christmas Eve, and went to bed the first time we were told, knowing we'd have to sleep fast in order to wake up in time for the predawn stocking checks.

Christmas morning was the most magical time of the whole year, and it began as soon as we could drag our sleepy parents from their bed. Apparently, we passed Santa's behavior checkups with flying colors, for gifts from the Great One—a doll buggy and roller skates and sled and doll house that looked a lot like the dog house Dad had been working on down the basement—were artistically arranged under the tree amidst the heaps of wrapped presents. We tore them open with excited abandon, despite Mother's pleas to be careful so the paper could be used again next year.

We dressed in our Christmas finery and ate our Christmas breakfast, cleaned up the Christmas mess and played with our new toys while we waited for Dad's relatives, more presents,

and Christmas dinner. The jingle of sleighbells from time to time warned us that even though we had gifts in hand, Santa was still keeping an eye on us.

Cousin Judy, carrying a box of Christmas tribute from her mother, heralded the arrival of the relatives and the second phase of our celebration, The grown-ups, in single-file order, solemnly navigated the icy patches between car and house bearing gifts, not unlike the wise men of old.

"Tom and Jerry?" Dad asked as he pressed a mug of the warm steaming drink into his guests' hands. We girls graciously brought the empties back to the kitchen, scraping off any of the egg and powdered-sugar batter that still clung to the sides of the mugs for our own consumption, while Judy gurgled down the rum remnants left in the bottoms.

The featured event of the afternoon was a repeat performance of the morning's gift opening activities. My sisters and I managed to maintain an acceptable-to-Mother level of decorum as we dutifully thanked each relative for the present, trying our best to express our joy and gratitude for the underwear and mittens we received. The grown-ups, in turn, acknowledged our gifts, assuring us that "it" was just exactly what they wanted.

Judy was more honest. "What do I want these dumb things for? I already got some mittens!" she yelled, dropping them on the floor. "What's this? A hat?" She put the funny-looking underwear on her head and stuck out her tongue at the embarrassed giver-of-practical-gifts before throwing it on the floor alongside the rejected mittens.

After the giving of gifts, the grown-ups returned to their adult conversations in the living room while Mom whipped the potatoes in the kitchen and Dad carved the Christmas turkey.

We lit the no-drip centerpiece candles on the table, summoned the guests to the dining room, and passed the food.

When dinner was over, Mother and my aunts cleared the dining room table and adjourned to the kitchen to do the dishes. My dad, grandma, and uncle eased themselves into the big soft chairs in the living room to let their dinners settle. We girls played with our new toys under the Christmas tree, while Judy alternated between directing our activities and making mysterious forays into the kitchen.

Feeling Christmas slipping away, I could hardly wait for the company to go home so my sisters and I could rekindle the mood of the morning, and embark upon phase three of the celebration—reliving the day far into the night.

Cousin Judy returned from her final kitchen excursion with a victorious smile on her face. She motioned for me to follow her into the bedroom. "My mother and your mother said you can come home with me and stay overnight."

Oh no! Not tonight! I thought in dismay. But one didn't say "no" to Cousin Judy.

The Night After Christmas I lay in Judy's big double bed with memories of the day racing through my mind while I babbled on about the hero of the day, Santa Claus. Judy lay next to me listening patiently for awhile, and then, unable to keep her secret any longer, confided, "There isn't any such thing as Santa Claus, you know."

No Santa? The warm happy thoughts streaming through my consciousness turned cold. If there were no Santa Claus, then who brought all those wonderful gifts?

"He's really your parents," Judy continued relentlessly.

An icy numbness grabbed my mind and froze out the protests that lay choking in my throat as Judy matter-of-factly related her own revelatory experience of unmasking the age-old fantasy.

"One Christmas Eve, before my dad died, I was supposed to be in bed sleeping, but I heard a noise in the driveway. I looked out the window and saw my parents unloading a lot of presents from their car. One of the presents was a tricycle. When I woke up Christmas morning, all the gifts were under the tree, and the tricycle had a tag on it that said, 'To Judy From Santa'."

I listened in silent disbelief, unable to deny the damning evidence of Santa's non-existence that poured from my cousin's mouth. I felt the world of my childhood crumbling around me. Then, sensing that she had gone too far, Judy stopped in midsentence and ordered me to "Go to sleep. Forget what I just told you."

I lay in bed, pondering the awfulness of Judy's story. A Christmas tune was softly playing on the bedside radio. The familiar words began to thaw the numbness from my brain.

He's making a list and checking it twice,

Going to find out who's naughty or nice.

Then, in a twinkling the truth became as obvious as lights on a Christmas tree. Santa only brought presents for <u>good</u> children! Cousin Judy was one of the <u>naughty</u> ones! Santa would never come to her house. Not in a million years! That's why my aunt and uncle played Santa Claus. They *had* to put her gifts under the tree themselves. Otherwise she wouldn't get any presents at all!

Secure in my new-found wisdom, I fell asleep to the tinkling of far-away sleighbells.

TURKEY TROT

Although my dad was born and raised in the city, he lived on a farm. In 1908 when he was five, his parents built their family home on 41st Avenue South, just off Lake Street in rural Minneapolis. Their outbuildings included a garage for the Model T, a barn for the cow, a coop for the chickens, and a garden shed. Dad's father was a printer who worked downtown for the *Tribune Newspaper*. His mother was a housewife, which meant she kept the garden, canned the vegetables, milked the cow, gathered the eggs, and killed the chickens for Sunday dinner. As Dad grew older many of these responsibilities fell upon his shoulders.

To paraphrase an old saying, "You can take the boy off the farm but you can't take the farm out of the boy." When Dad and Mother married they built a house in Nordeast Minneapolis.

During various summers Dad had a garden in the backyard, a garden across the street, a garden in the suburbs, a garden across town, a garden in the country, etc. I was his gardening assistant, as I preferred digging in the dirt to helping Mom clean and cook.

I thought a natural extension of our agrarian tendencies would be to have a chicken coop in the back yard, like the neighbor down the street, but Dad preferred to purchase his chickens live from somebody else's farm. He was a great believer in fresh meat, and while I sympathized with the hapless hens trussed up in our basement waiting for the ax, I have to admit they were a mighty tasty item on the Sunday dinner menu.

One year, however, he came upon a deal that was too good to pass up. A local farmer had an underweight turkey that he was willing to let Dad have for a bargain price. Since we would soon be in need of a turkey (it getting to be close to Thanksgiving time and all that), Dad struck a deal with the farmer and brought the bird home to fatten it up.

The dog had abandoned its house in the back yard long ago when it left for unknown reasons. Its old doghouse was the perfect size for our scrawny Thanksgiving Day turkey. Dad shoved the bird through the doorway and nailed slats every which way across the opening, leaving room at the top for the turkey to poke its head out and enjoy the view, and room at the bottom to shove in a dish of corn and some water.

As the eldest daughter, I was designated "Keeper Of The Turkey." It was my job to feed and water it every morning and every evening. I felt honored. After all, how many girls my age had an opportunity to make friends with a turkey?

The turkey, however, did not appreciate my efforts to establish a warm and loving relationship, even though it would

be of short duration. And it took exception to my attempts to minister to its needs, mercilessly pecking my fingers every time I poked the food and water in through the bottom of its makeshift cage. More corn ended up scattered on the ground outside the turkey coop than inside. However, I steadfastly honored my commitment and took to wearing gloves and bandaids. After all, this was to be our Thanksgiving Day dinner.

Thanksgiving week brought two surprises. We woke one morning to a beautiful snow that had fallen the night before, and to the sight of our Thanksgiving turkey strutting around the backyard, obviously enjoying its newly won freedom.

"Clarence!" my mother yelled to my father who hadn't yet gotten out of bed. "The turkey's loose!"

Dad peeled out of that bedroom faster than a speed skater on a banana skin. Throwing a coat over his pajamas and shoes on his feet, he raced for the back door, barreled outside, and commenced chasing that turkey from one end of the backyard to the other, skidding and slipping over icy patches of snow much to the amusement of the bystanders who had gathered to watch the show. Arms and wings outstretched Dad and turkey faced off, dancing round and round each other in a sort of surreal turkey trot. Finally, Dad saw his chance and with a flying leap that would do an NFL linebacker proud, he tackled that turkey.

When we came home from school that afternoon, there was fresh blood on the snow under the clothes pole where Dad had dispatched the bird. Although, by the end of its fattening up period the turkey was considerably more underweight than it had been originally, it tasted delicious.

MY THREE GRANDMOTHERS

The grandmother of my memories was short, plump, and full-bosomed with silver-white hair knotted into a bun at the nape of her neck during the day and released at night to cascade the length of her back. Although I saw her nearly every Sunday at the boring, but obligatory family dinners, we were generations apart. Our rare conversations were of the perfunctionary "yes" and "no" variety. We shared a name, "Irene," Grandma's first, my middle, but I was barely aware of the commonality for I addressed her formally as "Grandma Gossler." I was fifteen when my Grandma Gossler died, but I hardly knew her.

My father was the youngest of her five children and, as is often the case with youngest children, very close to his mother. In the five decades since her death, he has shared memories of

my grandmother with me and I feel that through these stories, I have come to know her as a real person, complete with human virtues and peccadilloes.

According to Dad, his mother was Goodness and Resourcefulness Incarnate. She raised her eldest son's child as her own when its mother died of consumption shortly after childbirth; She fed the hungry and housed the homeless; She provided refuge and a permanent home for an abused neighbor girl; She befriended foreign students at the University of Minnesota; and when my grandfather was severely injured in an accident, she successfully sold Venetian blinds door-to-door, keeping the family out of the poorhouse for the year he was laid up and unable to work. Dad's memoirs of his mother nearly had her earmarked for sainthood, except for one story he let slip in a moment of weakness—the story I call "Grandma and The Big Fish."

GRANDMA AND THE BIG FISH

It was a warm sunny day in mid-May, the kind of a day when fish, hungry from their winter fast, eagerly "hit" on anything landing on top of or in the water. Irene, my grandmother, was an avid fisherman. By this time of year she was chomping at the bit, or more precisely, digging up the worms, hoping for a chance to wave her old cane pole above the rippling lake water to tempt the famished fish below with the fat, wriggly lures.

My grandfather was a printer, working nights at the *Tribune* setting linotype for the next day's edition of the newspaper. Taking a day off to go fishing instead of sleeping was out of the question no matter how high the fish were jumping to the bait. On the morning of my dad's story, like every morning before it, Grandpa had come home from work, locked the Model-T in the garage, put the key in his pants pocket, pulled the shades down in his bedroom, draped his pants over the chair, and tucked himself into bed for his daily snooze.

This day, however, it was more than Grandma could bear. "Clarence," she said to my twelve-year old father-to-be, "Get the big screwdriver and come out back with me." By the time Clarence had screwdriver in hand, Irene had a ladder leaning against the garage. "Now Clarence," she said firmly in her no-nonsense I-am-your-Mother voice, "Unscrew these hinges on the garage door."

Obediently, Clarence loosened the hinges that held garage door to garage frame imprisoning the Model-T within. Together, mother and son caught the freed door and temporarily set it against the side of the garage. "Get in, Clarence" Irene ordered. "You steer, I'll push," and silently the Model-T made its way backwards down the dirt driveway into the street.

48

Clarence set the brake. Then he and his mother scurried back to the garage to rehang the door and hide the ladder lest Papa wake up and take a peek out the window just to satisfy himself that all was well.

"Think you can manage to drive this thing, Clarence?" Irene asked as the two of them got back into the vehicle. "I'd drive it myself if I didn't think it would attract undue attention, me being a woman and all."

"Sure, Mama. I've watched Papa drive it lots of times. You just crank it up and hop in. I'll do the rest."

Irene cranked up the black behemoth, and with Clarence at the wheel, the two of them bumped and jerked down the rutted road that led to the fishing spot that was calling her name.

They rented a rowboat from a lakeshore farmer who was kind enough to throw in two cane poles as part of the bargain. Irene located the can of worms she had dug before they left and

49

scooped the squirmy critters back into the can from whence they had spilled in the back seat of the car. Together, she and Clarence pushed the boat out into the dancing waters of the lake and settled themselves into a pattern of contentment—Clarence lazily manning the oars and Irene happily trailing her line out the back of the boat.

The sunnies and crappies were biting like mad and their dappled green and golden bodies started piling up in the bottom of the boat. Then Irene snagged a fish that nearly bent her cane pole double. The fish fought and she struggled to land the creature which turned out to be an admirable-sized bass. The only trouble was bass season hadn't opened yet. Torn between the promise of a bass dinner and the law, she opted for the former. The illegal bass took its place in the bottom of the boat along with its legitimate brethren.

"Mama!" Clarence protested. "What if you get caught? They'll put you in the pokey and Papa will find out for sure that we've taken his car!"

"Now Clarence," she scolded. "If all you're going to do is complain, you can stay home after this. Pass me another worm."

The day was well into afternoon—time to get the car back before Papa began to wake up and start looking for his dinner. Clarence was pulling up anchor when an official looking boat rowed up beside them. Manning the oars was the game warden. "Afternoon Mam," he said tipping his hat in Irene's direction. She was sitting with her back to him fiddling with her dress. "Having any luck?" he asked, eyeing the catch on the bottom of the boat.

Irene turned her head, smiled sweetly, and answered, "So, so," sweeping her hand over the day's catch in a broad gesture. The bass wasn't among them.

The game warden eyeballed the back of the boat which was also devoid of bass and said his goodbyes. Clarence resumed both his breathing and his struggle with the anchor, then put the oars in the oarlocks and rowed back to shore.

They beached the boat, bagged their fish in a gunnysack, and returned the cane poles to the farmer. Clarence could stand the suspense no longer. "Mama!" he demanded. "What did you do with that fish?"

Irene looked around. Satisfied there were no curious eyes looking their way said, "Clarence, you be a gentleman and cover your eyes until I say you can look."

Clarence did as he was told, except for the v-shaped peephole he formed between his second and third fingers. Unobserved by his mother who was preoccupied with the front of her dress, he watched her pull the contraband bass out from beneath her ample bosom and slip it into the fish bag along with the others.

June Irene Anderson

MOTHER HEN

April 24, 1995: Today I taught first grade. Being a kindergarten through grade 12 substitute, I'm not in first grade classrooms very often, so I was very pleased to see that the regular teacher had left me detailed instructions for conducting her class.

The first item on her list was to "turn the eggs." I spotted them on the counter between the crayon boxes and big paste jar—eighteen brown eggs cradled in a state-of-the-art electric incubator. As I took the cover off the glass-domed nursery and rolled its contents over to numbered side up, I thought back to another time and reflected upon my longstanding obsession with the egg and the tantalizing promise of life held within its shell. But most of all, I remembered my steadfast ambition to become a Mother Hen.

I grew up during the forties, a misplaced city girl who was fascinated with animals, especially those that popped out of a shell. My more fortunate cousins lived on a farm with a barn and a henhouse. Instead of buying all our groceries from the store, we city kin got our eggs by the case from their mother, my aunt, who raised chickens for some "extra chicken feed," as she liked to say.

Well, even at my tender age I knew a few things about the birds and the bees, and I most certainly knew the difference between store-bought eggs and farm eggs. Farm eggs were fertile. Store-bought eggs were not. Armed with that knowledge I was determined to fan the spark of life that lurked inside those temptingly fertile farm eggs.

For my first try at hatching out a brood I appropriated a half dozen eggs from a newly arrived egg case and smuggled them into an excelsior nest I had hidden in the fruit cellar under the basement steps. I waited and waited for the miracle inside those eggs to materialize. A few months later I abandoned that nest when I realized that the stone-cold eggs were probably not going to hatch. I would have to delay Mother Henhood for a while.

But I did learn something from that experience. I learned that eggs needed to be kept warm in order to turn into baby chickens. Shortly after my unsuccessful hatch attempt, opportunity knocked again and the deliveryman brought a new shipment of farm fresh and fertile eggs. This time I snitched just one of the eggs to test my new theory about hatching them.

Now the warmest place in our house was the double bed I shared with my little sister Patty. Patty and I usually spent the early part of our designated bedtime arguing and fighting about whose big toe had trespassed over the centerline of the bed. Our routine didn't vary the night the farm eggs arrived. At the close of our evening battle, when Patty lay contentedly snoring away, thumb in mouth, I took the egg from its hiding place in our bedroom and tenderly tucked it under my soft feather pillow, a logical substitute for the natural mother, I reasoned. Then I fell asleep.

I awoke with a start in the middle of the night. I couldn't believe it! The unthinkable! Patty had "done it" in bed! Indignantly I marched downstairs to my parents' bedroom to report this outrage. Mother couldn't believe it either, and she rushed upstairs to investigate my claim. She pulled back the bed sheet—and there it was—yellow slime with bits of eggshell scattered throughout. And there I was—trying to explain how an egg happened to find its way under my pillow.

Although Mother took pity on me and permitted me to "adopt" some baby chicks that had "followed" me home from the local feed/seed store, I still yearned to hatch out my own brood. That opportunity surfaced a dozen or so years later when I read an intriguing article in the *Picture Magazine* section of the Sunday paper. It was entitled "Make Your Own Incubator Out Of A Cardboard Box." I had just started teaching and I thought this would be a very worthwhile project for my fourth-graders. So my class and I appropriated a big cardboard box from the storeroom, hooked up a light bulb for heat, and filled a pan with water for humidity. After school I drove to Ghostley's Chicken Ranch near Anoka to buy one dozen fertile eggs.

The next morning the class and I placed the eggs in our newly constructed incubator and read about the day-to-day development of the embryonic chick. Every day we turned the eggs and crossed off on the calendar the time remaining until hatch day. Every Thursday we drew names to see whose lucky mom got to drive to school on Friday to take our inutero chicks home to baby-sit for the weekend.

The classroom tingled with anticipation as we approached the final countdown to Hatch Day. On the morning of the 21st day the children streamed off the school bus and tiptoed over to the incubator. One by one they peeked in. There lay the eggs, undisturbed, with nary a crack in them. The children took turns checking the incubator at frequent intervals during the day. The eggs remained dead white and intact. Well, this was supposed to be a learning experience so we discussed the possible reasons for our non-hatch and decided it was too early. They would hatch <u>after</u> not <u>on</u> the 21st day.

The 22nd day was a repeat of the day before. The children expectantly checked the eggs at every opportunity. The uncooperative eggs just lay there, mocking us in their pristine beauty.

Nobody said much about the eggs or baby chickens on the 23rd day, although a few hopeful souls did venture a glance in the direction of the incubator box from time to time. The classroom atmosphere, which had been so alive with the promise of new life, now hung heavy and glum with disappointment.

When the children left on the bus at the close of the school day, I got into my car and made another trip to Ghostley's. Their stock was kind of low, they said, but they would do their best for me. I carefully placed my purchase in the car and drove back to school. All the staff had left by now and no one saw me enter the building. I unlocked the door to my classroom, removed nine of the eggs from the incubator, and carefully placed the contents of my package inside the incubator.

I took the nine eggs home with me that night to find out why they were such duds. With some trepidation for fear of what I might find, I cracked them open, one by one. Out of each oozed a gooey slime, much like that mess my mother had found under the bedcovers years before, only riper. Not one of those eggs had developed even a hint of an embryonic life. I washed out the shells and put them back in the bag.

Arriving at school early the next morning, I put the eggshell halves back in the bogus incubator. When the children came, they carefully ignored and purposely avoided going near our failed project. During a quiet time, Nancy, who sat in the back seat closest to the cardboard box, became aware of some strange little sounds coming from it. Hesitantly, she got out of her seat, walked over to the box, and peeked in. She looked again and came running up to my desk. "Chickens!" she announced. "They hatched!"

Crowding around the box, my brood of fourth-graders counted nine little balls of golden fluff pecking amongst the broken eggshells. Mark, the class mathematician, did some calculations and stated that we had a 75 percent hatch rate which was even better than that of the commercial hatcheries!

Of course, the whole school had to come see the Miracle in Room 4-A. I modestly kept a low profile, not quite knowing what to say about the phenomenon. Then one of the other fourth grade teachers took me aside and fixed me with a penetrating hawk-like gaze usually reserved for errant children. "Are you sure these chicks were just hatched out last night?" she challenged.

"Oh yes," I stammered uncomfortably.

Her steely-blue eyes bored into mine. "Well," she harrumphed, hands on hips, "I was raised on a farm and this is the first time I've ever seen day-old chicks with pinfeathers!"

COMPUTER PANCAKES

Jack was a computer whiz. His bedroom looked like the Space Control Center at NASA. In it he had a computer, two monitors—color for games and green screen for high-resolution programs—-two disk drives, a phone modem complete with telephone, a mouse and a joystick, a printer, stacks of printout paper, and scores of floppy disks. With his computer he could design his own greeting cards, make posters and banners, write twist-a-plot adventure stories, draw pictures, solve math problems, check on the stock market, and phone his late-breaking news stories into the Outerapolis Junior High School newspaper.

With his joystick Jack could outdraw, outshoot, and outmaneuver any kid in his school. He had once cleared the screen of enemy invaders in 26 seconds flat and chalked up 15

bonus games for his effort. After that feat he was known as "Sure Shot" in computer game circles.

Jack's Grandpa Clarence lived on the near side of Innerapolis. He liked to sit in his recliner rocker and watch television game shows. But more than that he liked to cook. And most of all he liked to cook buttermilk pancakes—big delicious batches of them.

Every Sunday morning Jack was invited to Grandpa Clarence's house to help him and Grandma Lois eat buttermilk pancakes. But even though he saved up his appetite all week so he could eat lots of pancakes on Sunday, there were always plenty of pancakes left over. "Too bad we haven't anyone else to share them with today," Grandpa Clarence would say to Grandma Lois as he tossed the dog another pancake.

In a green and white house on the far side of Innerapolis lived Jack's Great-grandma Cora with her cat, Kitty. Great-grandma Cora liked to sit in her easy chair by the window watching the birds, working crossword puzzles, and waiting for friends to call her on the telephone. Although she liked to eat, she did NOT like to cook.

One Sunday morning while Grandpa Clarence was frying up Jack's ninth helping of buttermilk pancakes, Great-grandma Cora phoned to get some help with her crossword puzzle. "What's a seven-letter word meaning 'Mormon Monument'?" she asked.

Jack was too full of pancakes to think about monuments. "I don't know," he said, trying hard not to burp.

"Pancakes this morning?" asked Great-grandma Cora. "I can almost smell them. Wish you could phone me a few," she said with a laugh before hanging up.

While his breakfast digested Jack started thinking about on-line pancakes. "It only seems logical," he said to Grandpa

Clarence, "that if you can wire flowers, you should be able to phone pancakes."

That evening Jack began to tinker with his computer. "First I'll interface Mom's food processor with the word processor and then I'll connect Mom's microwave to the microprocessor. It should work just fine." He looked at his disk drives. "Well, I really don't need two." So he converted one of them into a dish drive for serving pancakes. Now he was ready to program a pancake.

The printout of the listing for the pancake program looked like this:

0025 PRINT "GRANDPA CLARENCE'S RECIPE FOR BUTTERMILK PANCAKES"

0050 PRINT "BEAT UP 2 EGGS WITH A ROTARY BEATER."

0075 PRINT "MIX IN 1 QUART BUTTERMILK."

0100 PRINT "ADD ¼ CUP SUGAR, 1 OUNCE MELTED BUTTER, 1 TEASPOON EACH SALT, BAKING POWDER, BAKING SODA. BEAT WITH ROTARY BEATER."

0125 PRINT "STIR IN 3 TO 3-1/2 CUPS FLOUR. MIX UNTIL BATTER IS BLENDED BUT STILL LUMPY."

0150 PRINT "RUB BUTTER IN FRYING PAN AND FRY AT 350 DEGREES. TURN PANCAKES WHEN LOTS OF BUBBLES APPEAR ON BATTER SIDE."

The next Sunday Jack invited Grandma Lois and Grandpa Clarence over to HIS house for buttermilk pancakes. "My treat this morning," he said. "Shall we adjourn to the bedroom for breakfast?"

Perched on the edge of Jack's bed, Grandma and Grandpa were puzzled when Jack put a program in the disk drive and turned on the computer. "Thought we were going to eat," said

Grandpa as he tried to lift himself up from the soft bed. "Why don't I just go down to the kitchen and fry up some pancakes while you play with your computer. Never could see much sense to those contraptions anyways."

"This isn't a game, Grandpa," said Jack. "It's breakfast."

The disk drive whirred and stirred for a while and delicious smells came drifting out of the computer. Words on the color monitor announced first that it was "MIXING" and then, after some more whirring sounds from the disk drive, that it was "COOKING." When "ALL DONE" lit up the screen, Jack typed "RUN" and a floppy disk was transformed into a sloppy dish when it was ejected from the dish drive filled with syrupy, buttermilk pancakes.

Grandpa Clarence was skeptical. "I don't care if a computer CAN land a spaceship on the moon," he said. "This must be some sort of trick. It can't really make buttermilk pancakes!"

71

"Just try 'em, Grandpa," urged Jack. "See what you think."

"Looks like buttermilk pancakes," said Grandpa Clarence balancing a sloppy dish on his knees. He touched them lightly with one finger. "Feels like buttermilk pancakes." He held a forkful up to his nose. "Smells like buttermilk pancakes," he said as he moved the fork down to his mouth. He chewed for a while, and then swallowed. "Tastes like buttermilk pancakes!" he proclaimed. "And they are delicious!"

Jack typed "RUN" 15 more times until they had all eaten their fill. Then he hit the escape key and the program was canceled. But there were lots of pancakes still left in the system just waiting to be eaten.

It was then that Jack had his 64-megabyte idea! With a series of complicated adjustments, he converted the phone modem into a food modem and calculated the number of bytes to a pancake. "Now to test it," he said. He called up Great-grandma Cora on the other side of Innerapolis. "Had breakfast yet, Great-grandma Cora?" he asked.

"No," she said. "I think I'll just fix myself a bowl of dry cereal when I get around to it."

"How 'bout some nice, delicious, syrupy buttermilk pancakes this morning?"

"Sounds good," she said. "You going to mail me a batch? You know they won't get here 'til Tuesday and by that time they'll be cold and soggy."

"Better than that, said Jack. "I'll phone you a batch immediately, piping hot and delicious. Now hang up and I'll reconnect you with my computer."

When Jack heard the connect beep, he typed "RUN" again, and the pancakes were transmitted over the phone lines right onto Great-grandma Cora's plate. Jack's invention was a success and Great-grandma Cora had the best breakfast she had eaten in years.

■■

Great-grandma Cora had been a businesswoman many years ago and she knew a good thing when she ate it. As soon as she had finished her buttermilk pancakes, except for the last bite that she gave to Kitty, she started phoning her friends and all the lonely old people, shut-ins, and folks who hated to cook, that she knew.

"Ethelyn," (or Rose, or Myrtle, depending on who she was talking to) "have I got good news for YOU! You know those delicious buttermilk pancakes my son-in-law Clarence makes? Now YOU can have them for breakfast, too. All you have to do is subscribe to our PHONE-A-PANCAKE service and they will be delivered piping hot to you every Sunday morning via your telephone. You don't even have to leave your house. Isn't that exciting?"

All Great-grandma Cora's friends, lonely old people, shut-ins, and hate-to-cooks were very enthusiastic about this new fast-food concept and signed up immediately. Soon PHONE–A-PANCAKE became so successful that Jack, Grandpa Clarence, and Great-grandma Cora had to incorporate into a business. Since the food modem had been Jack's idea and also his invention, he was made President of the Corporation and Chairman of The Board. Grandpa Clarence became Chief Cook and Bottlewasher, and Great-grandma Cora, because of her expertise in the business world, was appointed Head of Marketing and Regional Sales Manager. She was so busy taking orders that she hardly ever had time to watch the birds or work crossword puzzles anymore.

As the business grew, Grandpa Clarence's position of Chief Cook and Bottlewasher was phased out when the computer took over that operation. He was promoted to Head of Quality Control and, on the side, gave guided tours of the ON-LINE PANCAKE PRODUCTION PROCESS. Sunday mornings would often find him in the computer kitchen lecturing the hoards of interested visitors on the complicated technological techniques used in producing pancakes by computer.

Mondays through Wednesdays Jack used his computer to compute the profits from Sunday's sales. Thursdays through Saturdays he hooked the printer up to the computer and printed out lots of posters and handbills that said:

COMPUTERIZED PANCAKES

DELIVERED

ON-LINE

CALL

"PHONE-A-PANCAKE"

And every once in a while he'd phone an ad into the Outerapolis Junior High School newspaper along with a late-breaking news story. Business was booming.

Then one Sunday a terrible thing happened! Complaints started rolling in from all over! Instead of delicious, syrupy buttermilk pancakes, people were receiving all sorts of strange concoctions over the phone lines. One shut-in called to say that she was getting pelted with wads of butter and chunks of cooked eggs. A lonely old lady screamed to high heaven that she did not appreciate dodo bird feathers in her syrup. Even the

hate-to-cooks, who usually aren't too critical of other people's cooking, said the stuff tasted kind of funny, and Great-grandma Cora's friends called and politely, but firmly, canceled their contracts with PHONE-A-PANCAKE. Business was definitely off.

Grandpa Clarence launched a Quality Control test of the gooey globs that had been returned to him by dissatisfied customers for refunds. He sent a memo to Jack that said:

TO: JACK, PRESIDENT AND CHAIRMAN OF THE BOARD

FROM: GRANDPA CLARENCE, HEAD OF QUALITY CONTROL

RE: THE AWFUL PANCAKES

MY FINDINGS ARE THAT THE RETURNED PANCAKES DO NOT <u>LOOK</u> LIKE, <u>FEEL</u> LIKE, <u>SMELL</u> LIKE, OR <u>TASTE</u> LIKE BUTTERMILK PANCAKES. PLEASE FIND OUT WHY.

Jack booted up his computer and typed "RUN GRANDPA CLARENCE'S BUTTERMILK PANCAKES." The disk drive whirred and stirred as usual, but strange smells emanated from the computer, and the entire output consisted of gobs of gloop. This confirmed Grandpa Clarence's test results that something was wrong.

Jack's next step was to command: "LIST GRANDPA CLARENCE'S BUTTERMILK PANCAKES." The listing pinpointed the problem at once. It was in line 0100 which read:

"WAD ¼ CUP SUGAR, 1 OUNCE PELTED BUTTER, 1 TEASPOON EACH SOFT ACHING POWDER, BAKING DODO. EAT WITH NOTARY HEATER."

Clearly the program had developed Bugs! They had munched away at the bits and bytes, completely invalidating the Buttermilk Pancake Recipe Program.

"No problem," said Jack as he set to work to debug the program. "I'm not called 'Sure Shot' for nothing." Reaching for his trusty joystick, he chased the speedy little bugs up, down, and around the screen, but he couldn't zap a-one. Jack's joystick had finally met its match.

"A mouse!" he exclaimed. "Mice can outrun bugs!" He programmed the mouse to chase and catch the bugs, but the program developed an I/O error when the mouse became more interested in nibbling on the bits and chewing up the chips than

chasing and catching bugs. "Bad idea," said Jack and he escaped that program.

∎∎

On the far side of Innerapolis Great-grandma Cora had disconnected her telephone and gone back to working crossword puzzles. She was still trying to figure out "Mormon Monument" while Kitty stalked a grasshopper that had snuck in through a crack in the door. Great-grandma Cora watched the insect absentmindedly for a minute, then leaped out of her chair shouting, "Eureka!" (meaning 'I have found it!') She plugged her telephone back in and called Jack. "Seagulls!" she yelled into the mouthpiece. "Seagulls!"

"What about seagulls?" asked Jack.

"They ate the grasshoppers and saved the Mormons! That's why they erected a monument to them in Salt Lake City!"

"That's it!" exclaimed Jack. "Birds eat bugs—and they're fast! Thanks, Great-grandma Cora. I'll get right on it!"

Jack began to peck furiously at the keyboard. He typed horizontal lines and vertical lines all over the place until a high-resolution animated graphic of a huge, hungry seagull appeared on both monitors. He typed "RUN" and the seagulls flew across the screen like winged pacmen gobbling up every last one of the pesky little bugs. With the bugs banished, PHONE-A-PANCAKE was back in business—that was if they still had any customers.

Grandpa Clarence was eager to resume operations. He was getting tired of watching television. "After all," he said, "What's one more game show when you've seen them all?"

Great-grandma Cora wasn't too sure she wanted to call all her old customers back on the phone. She was afraid they might say 'no.' "But," she told Kitty, "if there is one thing I learned in

84

my days as a businesswoman, it was that NOT to ask is an automatic 'no'." With order pad and pencil in hand, she picked up the phone and gave them all a call. "Ethelyn (and Rose and Myrtle), I have wonderful news for you! New and improved Computer Pancakes are back by popular demand. Now YOU can be the first on your block to resubscribe to PHONE-A-PANCAKE!"

To Great-grandma Cora's surprise and delight, her customers had forgotten how awful the bugged pancakes had been and remembered, instead, how good the buttermilk pancakes tasted. Besides that, most of them told her they were getting awfully hungry and wanted to renew their subscriptions as soon as possible.

Business was better than ever. With orders pouring in from all over Innerapolis and Outerapolis, Great-grandma Cora knew that her crossword puzzle days were over. "Oh well," she said to Kitty. "When you've solved one crossword puzzle, you've solved them all."

THE DAY SASHA FOUND HERSELF

One day when Grandma was babysitting the grandchildren, Grandpa stayed home to work in the garden. Sasha stayed home to help him. Although Sasha was a very little dog, she was a big help. When Grandpa dug in the garden, Sasha dug in the garden. When Grandpa planted beans, Sasha planted her bone. When Grandpa took a break, Sasha chased the tennis ball he threw for her.

"Enough ball throwing, Sasha," Grandpa said after awhile. "Time to get back to work."

He hooked up the old garden hose to water the garden. He turned on the water. It squirted him right in the face. "Oh, oh," he said. "I better get a new hose. This one leaks."

Grandpa hopped into his big van and drove to the hardware store. He had forgotten all about Sasha. When he got back from the store, he hooked the new hose up to the spigot and turned on the water. This time it did not squirt him in the face. It worked fine. Grandpa watered the squash. He watered the tomatoes. He watered the beans. Then he remembered Sasha. "Sasha," he called. "Here Sasha. Come Sasha."

Sasha did not come. Sasha was missing!

"Oh, no! This is terrible!" said Grandpa. "Grandma will be very sad if she comes home and finds out I've lost Sasha. I must look for her."

He walked over to his neighbor's house. Mr. Brown was mowing the lawn. "Mr. Brown," said Grandpa. "Sasha is lost. Have you seen her?"

"I haven't seen her today," said Mr. Brown, "but yesterday she brought her ball over for me to throw."

Grandpa walked over to Mrs. Green's house. She was swinging on her swing. "Mrs. Green," he said. "Sasha is lost. Have you seen her?"

"Not today," Mrs. Green replied, "but she was sitting on my lap swinging with me yesterday."

Grandpa felt very bad. He walked back home and climbed into his big van. He drove slowly up and down the street looking for Sasha. He asked everyone he saw, "Have you seen a little black dog with curly fur?"

Nobody had seen Sasha. Sadly, he drove home. Sasha was lost. What would he tell Grandma?

Grandpa parked the van in the driveway, opened the door, and got out. Sasha hopped out right behind him. "Sasha! Where have you been!" he exclaimed. "I've been looking all over for you!" He thought a minute. "Oh, now I know! You jumped into the van when I wasn't looking and went for a ride to the hardware store. Then you rode around the neighborhood with me to look for you!"

Grandpa picked Sasha up and patted her head. "Thank you for helping me find you."

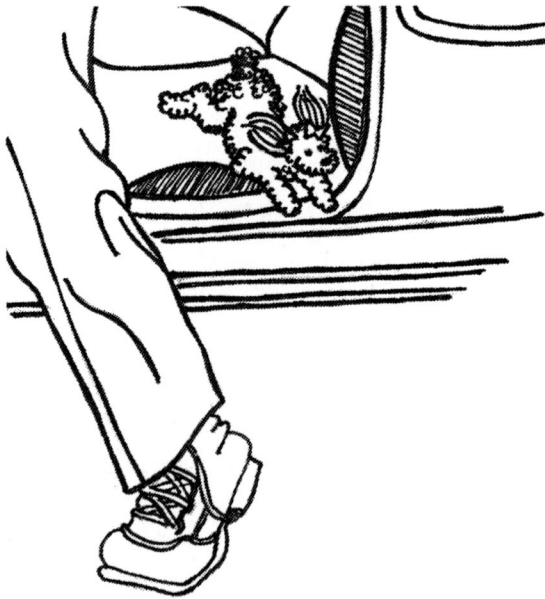

EPILOGUE

WHATEVER HAPPENED TO COUSIN JUDY?

Judy reached adulthood without any serious mishaps. Not too hard to understand since she was always in control of the situation. After high school her mother begged and pleaded with her to enroll at the University of Minnesota, but Judy was not interested. Instead she married the son of a college professor who became a college professor himself, moved to California, and successfully raised their four children as well as her husband's motherless siblings.

In preparation for Mom and Dad's 60th wedding anniversary celebration in 1996, we sisters asked friends and relatives to write a special memory of our parents. Cousin Judy shared the following:

INADEQUATE DEFINITIONS:

Not equal to that which is required to state what a word signifies.

UNCLE: *The brother of one's mother; the husband of one's aunt.*

This does not begin to describe the uncle who was always there for my mother and me; who walked me down the aisle 42 years ago.

AUNT: *The wife of one's uncle:*

This hardly does justice to the aunt who put up with me during my 'difficult years'.

FAMILY: *A group of persons connected by marriage.*

It's nice to know that no matter where you go or how long you are gone, you are still part of the family.

About The Author

Wife of one, mother of four, and grandmother of ten; June Anderson is a schoolteacher and writer. Her passions include theater, music, and her family. Mrs. Anderson holds degrees in Education, English, and Library Science from the University of Minnesota and the College of St. Catherine. Her part-time employment as a substitute teacher allows her to write monthly features for the arts page of the local newspaper, serve as vice president and membership chairman for the county arts alliance, and write the publicity for the local community theater. *Shades of Childhood* is one of two books she is publishing simultaneously. The other is a Civil War history co-authored with her great-grandfather.

About The Illustrator

Caryn Inderlee is a freelance artist of many talents. Her published artwork includes illustrations for two cookbooks and a coloring book. Her most visible public painting is that of a 12 foot tall mounted knight gracing the wall of the "Saints" hockey arena in East Bethel, Minnesota. Caryn's interest in the arts extends to other areas as well. An accomplished singer and actress, she is a regular performer in community theater. She puts her talents to work off stage as well, designing and constructing sets and props, painting backdrops and scenery, and doing the artwork for publicity. Caryn and the author have worked together in community theater for many years. This is their first collaboration on a book.

CPSIA information can be obtained
at www.ICGtesting.com
Printed in the USA
FSOW01n1444260615
8313FS